Series editor: CAROL BARRATT

CLASSIC
BALLET

Arranged for piano solo by Barrie Carson Turner

Chester Music

Contents

Dance of the Blessed Spirits
from *Orfeo ed Euridice*

Christoph W. Gluck (1714-1787)

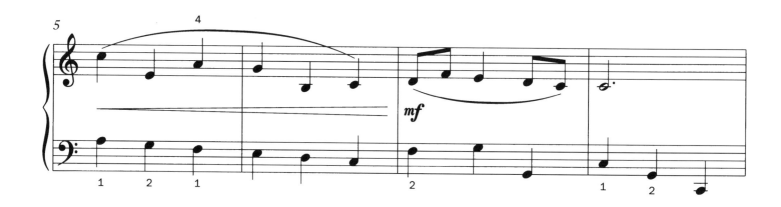

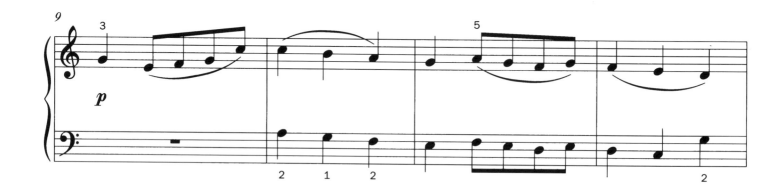

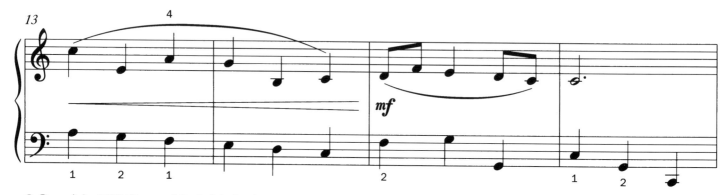

Entr'acte

from *Rosamunde*

Franz Schubert (1797-1828)

Dance of the Little Swans
from *Swan Lake*

Piotr Ilyich Tchaikovsky (1840-1893)

Waltz
from *The Sleeping Beauty*

Piotr Ilyich Tchaikovsky (1840-1893)

D.C. al ⊕ Coda   ⊕ CODA

Valse Lente
from *Coppélia*

Léo Delibes (1836-1891)

Tempo di valse moderato

Polovtsian Dance
from *Prince Igor*

Alexander Borodin (1833-1887)

Pizzicato Polka
from *Sylvia*

Léo Delibes (1836-1891)

16

Waltz of the Flowers
from *The Nutcracker*

Piotr Ilyich Tchaikovsky (1840-1893)

Dance of the Sugar-plum Fairy
from *The Nutcracker*

Piotr Ilyich Tchaikovsky (1840-1893)

Andante ma non troppo

March
from *The Nutcracker*

Piotr Ilyich Tchaikovsky (1840-1893)

Tempo di marcia viva

Ballet
from *Faust*

Charles Gounod (1818-1893)

Moderato con moto

D.C. al $\oplus$ Coda

$\oplus$ CODA

Czardas
from *Coppélia*

Léo Delibes (1836-1891)

Pas de Deux
from *Giselle*

Adolphe Adam (1803-1856)

Andante grazioso

Elite Syncopations
from *Elite Syncopations*

Scott Joplin (1868-1917)